PAUL J'S

50

WORST DAD JOKES

and other annoying forays into the
irrational world where only

a true DAD dares to go

mostly written

by

Paul Janson

Dedication: To my daughter Emma

Acknowledgement: For all those who helped with and supported this effort. They include, Mary and Emma Janson, Tom Sagui, Peter Amons, and many others too numerous to mention here, but all worthy of my gratitude.

The characters, events, institutions, and organization in this book are strictly fictional. Any apparent resemblance to any person, alive or dead, or to actual events is entirely coincidental. That's why it's so boring.

This material is a collection of my original jokes and some I've heard. I have edited the borrowed material when necessary. I have done this, not out of egotistical character, but out of respect. To improve the borrowed work is a sign of respect.

Author photo by Sarah McGrath

Copyright JM Publishing   January 22, 2023
ISBN: 978-0-9907424-9-4

First: Why am I writing a Dad joke book?

The editing is easier than it would be for a novel.

The constitutional issues:

Does the first amendment to the US Constitution include to tell dad jokes as free speech?

Maybe I should stop right here.

If it's "<u>free</u> speech" I might not be able to charge people for the book?

The second amendment to the United States' Constitution says I have the right *to keep and bear arms.*

Does that mean I can keep my bombs too?

Should I join the NBA, National Bomb Association?

Maybe it's a misprint and the founders intended it to be the right to *bare* arms.

The right to wear a tee shirt in public is important too.

It was handwritten ... in cursive! No wonder the Supreme Court has trouble interpreting it. No one can read cursive anymore.

Okay. Now the serious stuff.

How do you get two elephants into a car?

Start with a car that has one elephant in it, and put another one in.

What is *beyond* the bed and the bath?

Do you really want to know?

Don't people deserve some privacy?

Two peanuts went into a bar, and one was a salted.

Here's one to think about. Why is that last joke funny?

That's the shortest joke in this book. Only eleven words. Did you count them?

Here's a really silly question:

What's the sound of one hand clapping?

I don't know that answer, but I can show you the sound of one hand *slapping* a person who wastes my time asking a stupid question like that.

Do you know how to save a drowning person?

You can look it up on Gurgle.

My wife says that she enjoys making love, but it's hard to be sure.

Do all women laugh when they're having sex?

I don't understand why men don't want to wear masks during the pandemic.

It's easier than shaving every day.

How can someone figure out
my password when I can't
even remember it long
enough to write it down?

My daughter tried to explain,
but I didn't understand it.
Something about how dumb
dirt is.

Speaking of dumb as dirt:

Do you really want to live on Mars if Elon Musk is going to be your neighbor?

By the way, what does BTW mean?

I really sent this in an email to a copy editor OAP, (of all people.)

Real dads don't just tell jokes, they live them.

I really like texting and making up my own slang. ITTF.

I think that's funny.

Get it?

(5+5) + (5+5)

It could be four nickels, or it could be a paradigm.

(Pair 'a dimes)

Or maybe a palindrome.

I saw an ad to help people lose weight. It showed a picture of a chubby person, and then a thin person two weeks later.

Seriously, would you buy something from a person who needed two weeks to photoshop a picture?

No "Dad" joke book is complete without a New Year's Resolution joke, so here it is.

I make one resolution each year and I always keep it.

I resolve not to attend any New Year's Eve celebrations for the next 364 days.

My wife actually thought that one up, but she isn't a dad so she can't use it. It's definitely not a mom joke.

I showed this to my daughter to verify the quality of the content, which she did.

She said, "These are the worst jokes, Dad!"

I replied, "No. These are the worst *Dad* jokes, Daughter!"

Now for the quiz. These are two slightly modified quotes. Their original author's identity is revealed in novels I've written that can be purchased on Amazon for a very reasonable price.

First one: I'm not a very good cook. I can only cook two meals. One is shepherd's pie and the other one isn't.

It's not made with real shepherds either.

That's really two jokes, isn't it? I should raise the price for this book.

Last one: For people who like this sort of thing this is exactly the sort of thing they would like.

The answers are also at the end of this book, but you have to read the *whole* book to get to the end.

It might be easier to buy the novels.

I said to my wife, "You know all the great chefs are men."

She replied, "So are all the great busboys."

I do know how to cook tofu.

Throw it out and get some
real food to cook.

Speaking of Power Ball:

   (somewhere, someone must be speaking of Power Ball)

Why don't we ever read: "*Psychic wins the Power Ball! Again!*"

That was just the set up.

Here's the real joke:

Am I the only one who thinks
POWER BALL is just a little
obscene?

The lottery is my retirement plan.

Saving money is too expensive.

I am diversified though.

I buy lots of different games and in different states too.

Why do they call the lottery a "Game", like it requires skill to play?

I talked to my financial planner to make sure I had enough money to retire.

He said my best option was to die young. I'm working on it, but I may have waited too long.

I bought a Dad Joke book to help me write this book. I couldn't use any of their jokes.

They were too funny to be in my book.

I'm not going to get into the creation of the universe argument. That's not a dad thing, but the Big Bang Theory (the real theory, not the TV show) says a long time ago, everything was in one place. Then it started expanding, and the stuff collected to form galaxies, then the stuff in galaxies got together to form stars, but there was still a little stuff left over. That's us.

We are kind of like the pieces left over when you finish putting a piece of IKEA furniture together. The ones you can't figure out where they go, or what they're good for, or even whether they're important at all.

That is the longest joke in the book. Two pages. Just thought you'd want to know.

Was it worth all that reading?

How do we know that aliens are not one of the colors we can't see? There are a whole lot of colors our eyes can't see, like infrared and ultraviolet.

Those colors that are coming through the hole in the ozone layer.

So, there might be an alien standing right next to you that you can't see.

Of course, they probably can't see you either, so why did they come here anyway?

Everyone complains about how cold it is in winter and how hot it is in summer.

What do they want?

Too hot in winter and too cold in summer instead?

Why is summer hot anyway?

People say it's the weather, but I think it's the air conditioning.

When you turn on the A/C it takes all the hot air out of your house and dumps it outside, so it gets hot outside.

Next summer turn off you A/C. I bet the outside will feel cooler.

If people really believed
there is global warming,
they'd be figuring out where
the new beach front property
is going to be.

I've reached the stage in my life when dressing up to go to a party is combing my hair.

Does anyone who is reading this know how to count to 50, or can I stop at joke number 45?

Did anyone know we're on page 45?

Let me help you.

PAGE NUMBER 45 ←

For those of you who
checked to see if it really
was joke 45

You qualify for the
OCD OF THE YEAR AWARD

Why is it that a diamond is a woman's best friend, and a dog is a man's best friend?

Cubic zirconium is really a man's best friend. Until his spouse takes the ring to a pawn shop anyway.

I used to worry that when I got old, I'd get demented. As life becomes more complicated, I've begun to worry that I won't get demented soon enough.

Two alternative versions:

I used to worry that when I got old, I'd get demented. As life becomes more complicated, I've begun to worry that I'm already demented.

I used to worry that when I got old, I'd get demented. As life becomes more complicated, I've begun to worry that I have always been demented.

All these jokes make sense
except when they don't.
or
All these jokes are funny
except when they aren't.
or
None of these jokes both
make sense and are funny.
Things that make sense
aren't funny.

They're depressing.

My mother once told me that if I couldn't say anything nice, don't say anything at all.

She never spoke to me again.

I raise chickens so I can assure you, no chicken has ever worried about why they crossed the road or whether the egg came before they did.

Why are we worrying about it?

Are we trying to prove we're smarter than chickens?

They don't care who is smarter.

I heard the government is collapsing.

I was really surprised.

I didn't know we had a functioning government.

Where are they hiding it?

I'm retired now, which is why I have time to write this book.

I have no job to go to, and my wife and daughter take care of themselves.

Despite this, I spend more time trying to keep functioning than I did when I had a reason to keep functioning.

What do you call a deer with no eyes? No eye deer. (No idea)

What do you call a deer with no eyes and no legs? Still no eye deer. (Still no idea)

There's a third part to this joke that I can't print without changing the rating on this book, but you can guess what it is, Dick.

All the smart people in the pharmaceutical business are devoting their time to thinking up names for the drugs.

Elavil? Just saying that makes you feel happier.

Lopressor? My blood pressure is going down.

Viagra? That'll make you feel alive and growing.

Okay, so the first two are not really *dad jokes*, but I had to include them in order to justify printing the third one.

Speaking of hearing: Why is my voice the only sound my wife can't hear?

It's hereditary.

Our daughter can't hear my voice either.

That's funny because our daughter is adopted.

My Word Program just texted me: *I'm going to refuse to spellcheck your writing if you misspell voise one more time.*

My wife told me these jokes aren't funny.

So, I said, "Tell me a *Mom Joke*."

She said, "I'm talking to one right now."

(Cheap shot, but still funny)

My smart phone is getting surly.

It's correcting the spelling and punctuation in my voice messages before it will allow me to record them.

I didn't even know voice messages had punctuation.

Not everyone thinks these jokes are foolish.

Only the people who read them think that.

My mother always said her ancestors came over on the Mayflower, but I found out they missed the Mayflower and had to come on the Juneflower instead.

Immigration wasn't a big issue with the Pilgrims.

When I got married, I had to buy a new suit.

When my daughter got married, her fiancé had to rent a tuxedo.

He had to return the tuxedo, but it still cost him more to rent than I spent to buy my suit.

No wonder men want to avoid commitment.

Now I'm going to give this to my wife and daughter to edit.

All the jokes you don't see here are the ones they threw out.

I thought those jokes were really funny.

I can't argue with them.

It's a battle of wits and I'm unarmed.

.

Appendix A for amendments

Amendment I

Congress shall make no law respecting an establishment of religion, or prohibiting the free exercise thereof; or abridging the freedom of speech, or of the press; or the right of the people peaceably to assemble, and to petition the Government for a redress of grievances.

Amendment II

A well regulated Militia, being necessary to the security of a free State, the right of the people to keep and bear Arms, shall not be infringed.

This amendment is perhaps the most contested law in this country. It is only 27 words long, yet the legal judgements are hundreds of pages. Lawyers must get paid by the word?

Okay. The obligatory, dad attempt at education is fulfilled.

Appendix P for poetry

About chickens and my favorite

I sometimes think I'd rather crow
And be a rooster than to roost
And be a crow. But I dunno.

A rooster he can roost also,
Which don't seem fair when crows can't
crow.
Which may help, some. Still, I dunno.

Crows should be glad of one thing, though.
Nobody thinks of eating crow,
While roosters they are good enough
For anyone unless they're tough.

There are lots of tough old roosters though,
And anyway, a crow can't crow,
So maybe roosters stand more show.
It looks that way. But I dunno.

Anonymous

One final dad word:

Joyce Kilmer wrote:

I think that I shall never see
A poem lovely as a tree

Paul J wrote:

And that is why I'll stop at this
And not go on to finish it.

The words I put upon this page
Will fade and die with passing age.
The page on which they come to be
Was sadly made by killing a tree.

Appendix Q for Quiz

Ulysses S Grant once said: *I know only two tunes: one of them is Yankee Doddle and the other isn't.*

Abraham Lincoln said: *People who like this sort of thing will find this the sort of thing they like.*

About the Author

Paul Janson is a retired emergency medicine physician who has filled his retirement by pursuing his love of literary expression and his love of humor.

He has published six novels, two non-fiction works and a dozen children's picture books, all in just six years. He may have to go back to work just to get some rest.

In the meantime, he lives with his wife, Mary, of 48 years; a daughter adopted from Ecuador, and he is helping run a family-owned ice cream shop in Groveland, MA. *Jeff and Marias Ice Cream.*

Other books by Paul Janson include

Mal Practice a mystery of medicine and murder. Pediatrician Joe Nelson is being sued in a malpractice case involving the death of one of his patients, when he discovers that his patient was murdered, soon he becomes the next target.

With a Little More Practice: a sequel to Mal Practice. Joe and his friends are in Las Vegas when murder intrudes on their vacation. The victim is a young run-away and Joe can't ignore this even when he finds himself at odds with the police.

Scratch: a young adult novel of magic and cats. A magical cat saves lives by scratching people and two young sisters are the only ones who seem to realize just how special their cat is.

The Manuscript, a thriller of nuclear terrorism. A literary agent and retired police sergeant uncover a plot to detonate a dirty nuclear bomb when an inmate sends a query letter about a manuscript he has written.

Advance Directive: A sequel to The Manuscript. Someone is killing the patients in the local nursing home to get their inheritance.

The Ice Cream War a mystery of hot fudge and murder. The story of two rival ice cream shops and the body found in one of them. There is murder, humor, and a little romance in this story.

The Child In Our Hearts. A children's picture book about adoption and based on the belief that all children begin in the heart of their parents regardless of how they come to be in a family and regardless of what kind of family they become a part of. There are several versions of this book for different families. Some are available in Spanish as well.

Battles and Battleships, a narrative history of naval warfare from 1866 to 1905 Paul's first non-fiction work encompassing the development of the battleship and the lessons that can be learned and applied to our current time.

The Vice presidency A history of the fascinating people who filled the second highest elected office in this country.

www.ingramcontent.com/pod-product-compliance
Lightning Source LLC
Chambersburg PA
CBHW060534030426
42337CB00021B/4260